21st Century Skills Library

S0-BZY-909

COOL STEM CAREERS

WIND TURBINE SERVICES TECHNICIAN

WIL MARA

Published in the United States of America by
Cherry Lake Publishing, Ann Arbor, Michigan
www.cherrylakepublishing.com

Content Adviser
Charles Bartocci, PhD, Professor, Program Head, Wind Energy Technology, Dabney S.
Lancaster Community College, Clifton Forge, Virginia

Photo Credits: Cover and pages 1, 20, 22, and 28 ©William Perugini/
Shutterstock, Inc.; page 4, ©Stephen Bures/Shutterstock, Inc.; page 6, ©Riccardo
Piccinini/Shutterstock, Inc.; page 8, ©BESTWEB/Shutterstock, Inc.; page 11,
©Yobidaba/Shutterstock, Inc.; page 12, ©spirit of america/Shutterstock, Inc.;
page 15, ©Lichtmeister/Shutterstock, Inc.; page 16, ©Paul Glendell/Alamy;
page 18, ©Goodluz/Shutterstock, Inc.; page 24, ©TebNad/Shutterstock, Inc.;
page 27, ©nostal6ie/Shutterstock, Inc.

Copyright ©2013 by Cherry Lake Publishing
All rights reserved. No part of this book may be reproduced or utilized in any form
or by any means without written permission from the publisher.

**Cataloging-in-Publication data is available from the Library of
Congress.**
978-1-62431-003-4 (lib. bdg.)
978-1-62431-027-0 (pbk.)
978-1-62431-051-5 (e-book)

Cherry Lake Publishing would like to acknowledge
the work of The Partnership for 21st Century Skills.
Please visit *www.21stcenturyskills.org* for more information.

Printed in the United States of America
Corporate Graphics Inc.
January 2013
CLSP12

COOL STEM CAREERS

TABLE OF CONTENTS

CHAPTER ONE
WONDERFUL WIND

In the dead of night, the cell phone on Josh's nightstand lights up and begins to ring. He throws the covers back and grabs it, instantly awake. He's all but certain who it is, and he's

Some wind farms have hundreds of turbines.

right. It's the manager of the energy company he works for, calling to tell him one of the **turbines** has begun to malfunction. Josh is one of their best wind turbine services technicians, so he gets most of the emergency calls. He jumps out of bed, pulls some clothes on, and heads to his truck. All the tools he'll need are already in there.

It takes him about an hour to reach the **wind farm**, which was built in an open field in the middle of nowhere. There are 20 turbines altogether, standing in a neat row. Each turbine looks like a giant pinwheel spinning in a slow, almost lazy way. The fifth unit from the left is the one with the problem. Josh parks next to it. His partner, Sarah, has already arrived.

They put on their tool belts, open the door at the base of the turbine's tower, and check their harnesses and safety equipment. After making sure that they'll be safe when they reach the top of the tower, Josh and Sarah step into the elevator. As it goes up, Josh thinks again about how nice it is to have elevators in these turbines. At his last job, there were no elevators—just ladder steps attached to the tower's inside wall. It took about 20 minutes to climb them, and he was always exhausted afterward.

He and his partner reach the top and step out, aware that those lazily spinning **blades** are just a few feet away now. One wrong move and Josh or Sarah could sustain a very serious injury. The blades are on a rod called an **axis**, and the axis runs into a large box called a **nacelle**. Josh believes the nacelle is where the problem lies. Crouching down, he opens it to reveal a dizzying array of gears and electric **modules**. Sure enough, one of the modules has failed. It is the one designed to receive wind speed information. When it failed, the turbine shut down. Josh knows his employer is relying on him to fix it as soon as possible—the longer it stays broken, the more money the company loses. But he's replaced electric modules before and knows exactly what to do.

Wind techs ensure that each turbine on a wind farm works properly.

Josh and Sarah head back down to the truck to get the replacement part. On the way, Josh calls the manager and says the unit will be functioning again within the hour. When he steps out of the tower, a cool wind blows on his back. *That's what keeps me in business*, he thinks with a smile.

■ ■ ■

Many people believe that using wind as energy is something relatively new. But humans have been taking advantage

21ST CENTURY CONTENT

Wind is an attractive form of energy for a variety of reasons. First, it is clean—there are no dangerous by-products. Second, it is renewable, which means it's unlikely to ever run out. Third, it is very easy to acquire, since the wind blows in many places, and turbines can be built in almost any open, unused area. And fourth, it is cost effective and rarely more expensive than other forms of energy. Wind power provides only a fraction of the world's electrical needs at the moment, but more turbines are being built every day. Many experts predict wind will one day become one of the most common sources of energy.

of it for centuries. Boats used sails to capture the wind more than 5,000 years ago. Some of the earliest known windmills were built in present-day Iran around the seventh century CE. These windmills were used to pump water and grind grain. Europeans began using windmills in the 1100s, also to serve farming needs.

Wind turbines are slightly different from windmills. Windmills have traditionally been used to serve agricultural needs.

Wind turbines contain complex machinery that allows them to turn wind power into usable electricity.

Turbines, on the other hand, convert wind power into electricity. The first turbines were built in the late 1800s in Europe. The first large-scale turbine used to generate electricity in the United States was the Smith-Putnam turbine, which went into service in Vermont in 1941.

A wind turbine is basically a tall pole, called the tower, with a set of spinning blades at the top. The blades are attached to a round piece called a **rotor**. The rotor turns on an axis, which extends back into a nacelle. Within the nacelle are the gearbox and the **generator**. The generator converts wind energy into electricity and then sends it through transmission cables that run down the tower. From there, the electricity runs through more cables, eventually ending up in people's homes, in offices and stores, and so on.

Wind turbines are being built all the time, usually at new wind farms. These are wide-open areas that house dozens—and sometimes hundreds—of turbines for the sole purpose of producing electricity. Today, there are hundreds of thousands of turbines being used in nearly 100 countries around the world. Along with the amazing growth of wind power comes the need for qualified people to keep the turbines in working order. Such people are known as wind turbine services technicians, but they often go by "wind techs" for short.

Wind techs don't just repair turbines. They also perform inspections and routine maintenance. There are more parts to a turbine than you might imagine. The nacelle alone contains an amazing number of parts. Each part is essential to keeping a turbine running efficiently. A wind tech has to be familiar with all of them to be able to pinpoint the cause of a problem and figure out how to fix it in a very short time. The job is challenging but also very rewarding. Perhaps best of all, a wind tech is an important member of one of the most rapidly developing industries in the world.

Do you have what it takes to be one?

Wind techs travel to different wind farms to make sure their turbines are always in peak working condition.

CHAPTER TWO
GETTING THE JOB

Because the job is relatively new, there is no "standard" way of becoming a wind tech. Companies that

Vertical-axis turbines are shaped differently than the more common horizontal ones.

hire wind techs do, however, look for people with certain skills and experience.

One skill is mechanical ability. If you're the type of person who's good at handling tools and taking things apart and understanding how they work, then you could become a wind tech. Also useful is a basic knowledge of electrical systems. Remember that wind turbines not only generate electricity but also have many electrical parts. That makes a basic understanding of electrical devices such as generators invaluable. Experience in the electrical field will help even more. Knowledge of **renewable energies** in general, and wind power specifically, is also helpful. Employers prefer applicants who have taken the time to learn about the wind industry.

Most important, of course, is knowledge of wind turbines and how they function. There are several different types of turbines. The most basic kinds are vertical (the axis is set vertically) and horizontal (the axis is set horizontally). However, they all operate similarly and possess the same key parts. Solid knowledge of how turbines operate will greatly improve a person's chances of becoming a wind tech.

As the demand for wind techs grows, so does the demand for formal education in the field. Some schools offer programs designed to teach skills a wind tech will need. These programs are usually found in either community colleges or vocational/ technical schools. Most result in a one-year certificate or a two-year degree. Students learn about basic turbine design and routine maintenance tasks. They also study how to detect and diagnose problems early, how to respond to a problem efficiently, and how to use the relevant equipment.

A one-year certification program focuses almost exclusively on turbine-related education. Two-year programs usually include general-education subjects. Some schools provide students with actual turbine equipment on which to practice. A prospective wind tech should also seek education in basic mechanics and electronics. This knowledge will give them an edge over people who don't possess such training. Furthermore, if you find your interest in wind turbines fading, you can still apply mechanical or electrical training to a variety of other professions.

Personality also plays a role in whether becoming a wind tech is the right choice for you. Perhaps the most obvious trait you need is an enjoyment of mechanical things. Another important trait is being comfortable working by yourself. There are times when a wind tech interacts with others, but a tech is very often alone. A wind tech may travel on quiet roads in the middle of the night. The same holds true for maintenance work and routine inspections. These are often one-person jobs requiring the tech to go from site to site, turbine to turbine, collecting information and making minor adjustments. To that end, wind techs also need to have the discipline and focus to motivate themselves.

Knowledge of tools and mechanical devices is important for anyone who hopes to work as a wind tech.

A wind tech must be the type of person who pays close attention to safety. Wind techs often work at the top of turbine towers, so a fear of heights will definitely be a problem! Turbine equipment is very powerful, with many moving parts and powerful electrical currents. One absentminded mistake can cause a serious injury or even death. Wind techs work in very tight spaces, such as inside a nacelle. There is very little room to turn around, and crouching or kneeling will be

Wind techs often work high above the ground.

required. And as you already know, a wind tech can be called upon at any time of the day or night. He or she has to be ready to go at a moment's notice. The best people, therefore, are those who prefer something outside of an ordinary "nine-to-five" job.

LEARNING & INNOVATION SKILLS

A wind tech must enjoy traveling. Turbines are usually in remote locations with few or no people. A tech may have to travel hundreds or even thousands of miles to reach them. Wind farms may be in desert regions, atop mountain ranges, or offshore in the ocean. Techs sometimes have to board a ship or even a helicopter! They also endure just about any weather condition imaginable. Remember, a malfunctioning turbine means lost electricity for the public and lost money for the company. A tech may end up trekking through raging rainstorms, driving blizzards, or choking heat to keep things running.

21ST CENTURY SKILLS LIBRARY

CHAPTER THREE
DAY TO DAY

A wind tech performs two main duties daily: routine tasks and repair work. Routine tasks include inspections and general maintenance. These take up the bulk of a

Wind techs keep careful track of which turbines need work and which ones are functioning properly.

tech's time and are intended to prevent problems from occurring in the first place.

Inspections require a tech to visit each turbine that has been assigned to his or her care. The tech has a checklist and goes through each item thoroughly and patiently to assure that all aspects of the turbine are working properly. This includes mechanical, electrical, and **hydraulic** parts and systems. The tech makes sure that all parts are tight and in good working order, transmission lines are clear, and gears are fully oiled. All **sensors** are checked to ensure they are correctly adjusted. Communications devices must be operating properly, because if there is a breakdown in communications between a turbine and its monitoring systems, the people who watch for problems will not know about them. A tech also takes readings from a variety of monitoring devices, which give the tech a picture of the turbine's health. This information is then passed along to the company that owns the turbine.

As for routine maintenance, a tech occasionally has to replace small parts that are near the end of their expected life span. It's better to replace a part when it has a little life left in it than after it actually breaks down. A tech checks various fluids that keep parts cool or movable, adding or replacing them as needed. The tech may also be responsible for the routine upkeep of substations, which are not a physical part of the turbines. Substations are located on the wind farms and help manage the flow of electricity that the turbines produce.

In terms of repair work, an experienced wind tech knows any part on a turbine can break down at any time. In fact, because so many of the parts are constantly in operation, each part will break down sooner or later. Rotor blades sometimes develop cracks or warps. Electronic parts burn out, and lines become frayed or fractured. Turbine processing systems develop bugs and glitches. Damage can also occur to the tower itself. A turbine will sometimes have to be shut down

Wind techs often carry laptop computers when they are on the job.

before repairs can be done. This is to assure the safety of the wind tech and to prevent the problem from getting worse. Sometimes a problem is so severe that the tech cannot handle it alone. In these cases, he or she contacts the employer and requests assistance.

A wind tech uses many tools that are common in other mechanical professions such as plumbing and carpentry. A variety of hammers is needed, and can include a claw and ball-peen, as well as different types of sledgehammers. Wrenches are also required, particularly when working within the nacelle. The most common wrenches are open-ended and socket. The best for wind techs are torque wrenches, which have indicators showing how much force, or torque, is being applied during use. This is because some of the equipment they work on is delicate. Too much torque could cause major damage. Wire strippers are another invaluable part of the tech's tool collection. These allow the tech to strip the plastic coating off wires. Then the wires can be connected with other wiring or be wrapped around contact points to supply energy to a device. A variety of screwdrivers is needed, too.

Wind techs use a variety of technological devices. A computer is a necessity, just as it is with so many other professions today. The best kind for a wind tech is probably a laptop or other portable system, as a tech is on the road frequently. Similarly, a cell phone with reliable service is a must. The tech needs to stay in touch with the employer and with other tech

21ST CENTURY SKILLS LIBRARY

people from time to time. The cell phone should be paired with a hands-free headset. The best headsets are wireless, because wires can get tangled on things and cause problems. Another important device is a **multimeter**, which detects electrical currents. It usually comes with small wired devices that can be applied to surfaces. The devices read whether a current is present, what its relative strength is, and so on. A tech also uses an **oscilloscope**, which monitors the changes in an electrical current. An **infrared tester** helps the tech determine the presence of dangerous heat buildup in parts of the turbine.

Hard hats and other safety equipment protect wind techs from injuries.

LIFE & CAREER SKILLS

A portable toolbox to carry tools from site to site is a must for a wind tech. A tech will benefit from wearing a tool belt, as well. In the tool belt are the tools the tech needs for a specific job. It also frees up the tech's hands when the tools aren't being used.

Most equipment used by a wind tech is purchased by the tech. Companies do not provide tools or equipment. The upside to this is that most of these tools serve other uses outside the job. Because the tools belong to the tech, they can be used for personal tasks such as household repairs.

Safety gear is perhaps the most important equipment a wind tech uses. This includes a hard hat, gloves and boots, elbow and knee pads, and ropes and harnesses for working high up. Ropes and harnesses are particularly important. One slip while working at the top of a turbine could cost a tech's life. Safety is an important part of a wind tech's job. But with preparation and awareness, a tech can avoid getting hurt and get on with the task at hand.

CHAPTER FOUR
BLOWING INTO THE FUTURE

P erhaps the most attractive aspect of being a wind tech is taking part in an industry that will probably grow by leaps and bounds. During the first three months of 2012, the United States generated more than 4 percent of its electric power

Wind power will likely become a more important energy source in coming years.

on wind farms. In the 2000s alone, the amount of electricity that was generated by wind energy increased by more than 50 percent. Because wind energy is basically free and will always be available, more companies are finding it wise to invest in turbine construction. With the human population constantly growing, the demand for inexpensive electricity will also grow. The more turbines go up, the greater the need will be for people who can keep them running.

21ST CENTURY CONTENT

About 100,000 people currently make their living through the wind power industry in the United States. Most of these people work on, or in association with, wind farms. Wind farms can be found in many locations around the United States, with most in the middle third of the nation. Some states, such as Florida, use almost no wind power. Others rely on it for a sizable portion of their energy needs. Iowa, for example, uses wind for about 20 percent of its electricity. Texas and California are also major consumers of wind power. Overall, wind is the most commonly harvested form of renewable energy—something to think about when choosing a green career.

21ST CENTURY SKILLS LIBRARY

The pay for wind techs varies tremendously. Because it is a relatively new profession, it has no set scale. On average, however, a wind tech makes from $15 to $35 an hour. Where a person lands within that range depends on a number of factors. Experience in wind energy is useful, since people who have already worked as wind techs are in very high demand. Experience in related fields, such as electronics or mechanics, can also increase pay. So can schedule and travel flexibility. Sometimes techs are hired for temporary projects. Then the pay can be a little higher than normal, depending on the work required.

Wind techs who have permanent, full-time positions will probably receive health benefits, life insurance, and vacation and sick time. They may even receive a pension, or retirement, plan. Those who are part-time, in temporary positions, or freelancers working for themselves may not receive these extras. The wind techs who command the greatest pay are not only those with the most experience but also those who take the time to keep up on the latest trends and developments in turbine technology. And this technology will certainly continue to evolve.

Clean, renewable energy is here to stay. The awesome power of the sun, wind, and moving water may provide the solution to producing nearly unlimited energy that causes little harm to the environment. A skilled and experienced technician in any of these fields will be valuable to the

Experts predict that there will be many jobs for wind techs in the future.

companies that harvest these resources and to the public. If you're a responsible, motivated person who likes working with your hands and being on the cutting edge of an exciting new field, then becoming a wind tech just might be for you.

Will you be a part of the renewable energy revolution?

SOME WELL-KNOWN PEOPLE IN WIND TECHNOLOGY

Ulrich Hütter (1910–1990), a German inventor, made enormous improvements in turbine design. His research involved blade material, width, number, and mobility. He also experimented with allowing movement in the rotor hub. This decreased the amount of stress a sudden gust of wind caused on the turbine, allowing parts of the turbine to last longer before having to be replaced.

Poul la Cour (1846–1908) was a Danish meteorologist, teacher, and inventor. One of his main projects was windmill design. For years, he worked on improving blade and rotor design, and power generation. In the 1890s, he successfully produced electricity using a windmill, creating the most practical wind-powered design of his time. His work led to windmill generators being built in farms and towns across Denmark.

Palmer Cosslett Putnam (1900–1984) was a geologist and engineer. He first studied turbine design and power generation in an effort to cut electricity costs at his summer home. After years of research and testing, the S. Morgan Smith Company used Putnam's designs to construct the Smith-Putnam turbine. Completed in 1941, the turbine was the largest of its time. The turbine was forced to close down in 1945 because of mechanical issues and supply shortages during World War II (1939–1945). But Putnam's designs improved turbine technology significantly and changed the way people thought about wind power.

GLOSSARY

axis (AK-sis) the rod on which a turbine's rotor turns

blades (BLAYDZ) the flat, wide paddles attached to a rotor in a fan or turbine

generator (JEN-uh-ray-tur) a device that converts one form of energy into another

hydraulic (hy-DRAW-lik) powered by liquid moving through pipes under pressure

infrared tester (in-fruh-RED TES-tur) a device that detects the presence of electromagnetic radiation

modules (MAH-joolz) separate units that can be joined to others to make things such as machines and buildings

multimeter (mul-TIH-muh-tur) a device that measures the properties on an electrical circuit

nacelle (nuh-SEL) a streamlined enclosure that contains many of a turbine's mechanical and electronic parts

oscilloscope (a-SILL-uh-skope) a device that monitors changes in a fluctuating electrical current

renewable energies (ri-NEW-uh-bul EN-ur-jeez) forms of energy that are produced by nature and are unlikely to ever run out

rotor (ROH-tur) the part of an engine or other machine that turns or rotates

sensors (SEN-surz) instruments that detect and measure changes and transmit the information to a controlling device

turbines (TER-buhnz) engines powered by water, steam, wind, or gas passing through the blades of a wheel and making it spin

wind farm (WIND FARM) a windy place with a lot of wind turbines for generating electricity

FOR MORE INFORMATION

BOOKS

Fitzgerald, Stephanie. *Wind Power*. New York: Chelsea Clubhouse, 2010.

Hansen, Amy S. *Wind Energy: Blown Away!* New York: PowerKids Press, 2010.

Jacobson, Ryan. *How Wind Turbines Work*. Mankato, MN: Child's World, 2012.

Spilsbury, Richard, and Louise Spilsbury. *Wind Power*. New York: PowerKids Press, 2012.

WEB SITES

Alliant Energy Kids—Wind Power
www.alliantenergykids.com/EnergyandTheEnvironment /RenewableEnergy/022397
This site has a lot of great basic information on wind power, including some detailed diagrams of a wind turbine and plenty of interesting facts.

Energy Kids—Wind
www.eia.gov/kids/energy.cfm?page=wind_home-basics
Check out this page to find great information on how wind energy is used in the United States. Read details about wind farm locations, maps, statistics, and more.

Kids & Energy—Wind Energy
www.kids.esdb.bg/wind.html
Find plenty of basic information, as well as games and projects that are easy and fun. This site also has some historical information and a few excellent diagrams.

21ST CENTURY SKILLS LIBRARY

INDEX

ABOUT THE AUTHOR

Wil Mara is the award-winning author of more than 130 books, many of which are educational titles for young readers. Further information about his work can be found at www.wilmara.com.